AF448014

I LOVE YOU ALL DAY AND ALL YEAR

Jack rose

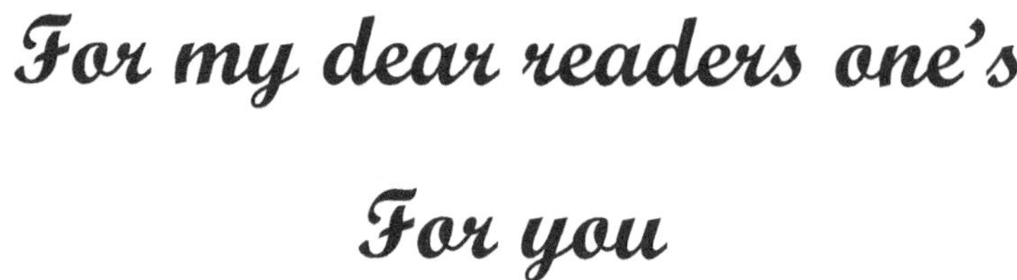

Trust your children

Give your children time to do their experiments,

Don't do things for them.

Yet we are often tempted to do it for them, to urge them to take action or we do not take the time to let them repair their clumsiness.

When I'm in a hurry or tempted to do something in my daughter's place because I think

"What is more urgent than
watching her do her own
experiences?"

"If you do it for you, you'll both win
three minutes. But what better
way to do it instead than to let her
learn? »

I often refrain from intervening
when she screws the cap upside
down or puts her jersey in front/
behind. I tell myself that it is by
making mistakes that she will learn
and develop her autonomy, that
she will take confidence in herself.

How can a child learn to dress
alone if his parents dress him every
morning to save time? How can a
child learn to use a glass of water if
his parents systematically serve
him for fear that he will spill it?

By doing it in the shoes of our children, we put them in a situation of frustration and dependence. From an early age, they can find a solution to the problems of their daily lives.

Think about how they learn to put their coats on at school (upside-down jacket): this method is not orthodox but it works! And they will have time to learn how to put their jackets properly, I've never seen any adult put his jacket upside down on the floor before putting it on ! We are transmitters, switchers, learners.

Let's trust our children!

Let's give our children time!

Let's let them find "their" solution!

Let them spill their glass!

Let them put their jerseys upside down!

Let's drop them so they get better!

But let's not forget to ask them questions to guide them to the right path!

Let's take a caring attitude and ask them, "How can you fix it?"

CHAPITRE 1

5 keys to give your child confidence

1-Appealing to your "part-who-knows-everything"

The unconscious, explained by the American psychiatrist Milton H. Erickson, is a "great store of solutions and resources" in which the individual sources his resources to solve his problems. It contains our family history over several generations, and part of the collective unconscious, that is, all human experiences since the dawn of time. The child also owns a "part-who-knows-everything," as Lise Bartoli has renamed it. She knows her anxieties, her desires, her feelings, but also the solution to her difficulties. «

An overly shy child is unable to explain why he is afraid to reach out to others, she observes. Questioning him about it makes him uncomfortable, reasoning him is insufficient. To change his behavior in-depth, one must go to the field of the unconscious. The method is playful, direct, and effective because it addresses its creative part, which has a positive capacity for transformation. »

The aim here is to materialize this "part-who-knows-everything" to make it more familiar and to summon it easily. The child can choose an animal, a character, a small object, or a "twin". The parent then invites him to ask for advice and solutions to this "part-who-knows-everything" to face his small difficulties. Then asks her child, but without forcing him to answer, which she advised him to do. The therapist sees how surprised parents are of the richness and relevance of the proposed solutions. In fact, they regain their trust as parents, and confidence in their child's resources is strengthened.

2-Guide him to his "magic world"

This key is to take the child to a world of well-being, where he feels confident. The goal: to strengthen his inner security, to help him create a space of positive transformation, and to awaken his senses to promote the encounter of the tale with his unconscious. This tool has the advantage of acting faster than relaxation, which it can later replace with its "magic world" as soon as it has consistency.

It is first suggested that the child close his eyes and choose his means of locomotion: horse, rocket or flying carpet, whatever. If he plays the game, it means he is already ready for change; otherwise, it's better to try again later. The parent then invites him to describe this magical world, emphasizing his feelings: "Is it a forest or a beach? Is it hot? Are there animals...? He can be encouraged to change details so that his world becomes truly "tailor-made" for him. It is important that he takes his time, that he sees himself and feels himself evolving in this new personal space to properly appropriate it. Finally, he was asked if he had "arrived" and "well settled".

3- Practice visualisation

irThe visualization consists of offering the child a mental image that speaks to the unconscious and then suggesting that the child transform it in a positive way. He then understands that he can act on his life, his emotions. Imagine a child who is afraid of the dark, he can create a fearsome monster, then transform it so that it becomes harmless, with a smile or a ridiculous hat. Visualization is an easy exercise to set up and very effective because the child is active. He will also be able to practice it alone later, by summoning his mental image when needed.

Another who has created a soothing and protective "sleep bubble" to combat insomnia can summon her if a new difficulty in falling asleep arises. "Don't forget your sleep bubble!" his parents will remind him. Stress ball to throw in a well, door of the future that leads to successes, tree of secrets ... The important thing is that the child becomes aware of both his "healing" resources and the trust that his parents have in them. It is not a question of developing a magical thought in him, but rather of showing him that he can act positively on his envonment.en needed.

4- Help him relax

Body relaxation is a very relevant tool for overcoming physically expressed difficulties, such as stress, chronic impatience, or tantrums. It also allows you to relax your mind and settle in a state of daydreaming, ideal for practicing visualization or hosting the metaphorical tale. The parent suggests that the child sit comfortably or lie down next to him in a quiet place, with or without a softie. He asks her to breathe through her stomach - inflate her belly on the inspiration, empty him on the exhalation - by setting an example for him, both to guide him and to relax. With his eyes closed, he makes her take

conscience des différentes parties de son corps – « Sens-tu ton pied gauche, ta main droite ? Sont-ils chauds, froids, lourds, légers ? ». Il lui raconte ensuite un moment de sa propre vie où il s'est senti bien et suggère à son enfant d'en faire autant, en insistant sur ses sensations tactiles, visuelles, olfactives…

If he lacks imagination, he can also tell a film he loved. By reliving these pleasant moments, children and parents will gradually change their state of consciousness. Metaphors will arise on their own, and the child's "part-who-knows-everything" will be available for viewing or storytelling. Once the relaxation has been mastered, the child will be able to practice it alone, before a stressful school event, for example.

5- Create your tale.

Fear of the dark, sadness, jealousy: all the difficulties of childhood can find their resolution in tales, which speak of them without naming them. The child unconsciously identifies with the wolf-threatened sheep without making the connection with his anxiety. Metaphor, the language par excellence of the unconscious, speaks directly to him. The child understands that he has the solution since the animal survives without the help of the shepherd.

The ideal is to invent a tale "just for him", which is inspired by his problem, but metaphorically. It is not a question of telling the story of a prince who pees in bed, but that of an overflowing river, for example. The canvas is always more or less the same: the hero can be a child, an animal, an object, which encounters pitfalls and overcomes them alone, thanks to a quality that he did not know to possess. The outcome is always positive. For the rest, just let your imagination run wild You can reread a few tales to reactivate it, or open a book at random, put your finger on one word, and then on another, with the problem of your child in mind. One can then invent a story from these words, even wacky, even very simple. This playful writing taps into our unconscious.

The latter is itself in symbiosis with that of our child since we share the same family history, the same universe. It is, therefore, more effective than traditional tales, with universal virtues. That's the difference between tailoring and ready-to-wear.

Thank you

NOTE

www.ingramcontent.com/pod-product-compliance
Lightning Source LLC
Chambersburg PA
CBHW071256140726
47996CB00007B/2863